Market Socialism: A Scrutiny
'This Square Circle'

ANTHONY DE JASAY

IEA
Institute of Economic Affairs
1990

First published in March 1990
Second Impression February 1991
by
THE INSTITUTE OF ECONOMIC AFFAIRS
2 Lord North Street, Westminster, London SW1P 3LB

© The Institute of Economic Affairs 1990

Occasional Paper 84

All rights reserved

ISSN **0073-909X**

ISBN **0-255 36232-3**

The Institute gratefully acknowledges financial support for its publications programme and other work from a generous benefaction by the late Alec and Beryl Warren.

Printed in Great Britain by
GORON PRO-PRINT CO LTD, LANCING, WEST SUSSEX

Set in Berthold Plantin 11 on 13 point

Contents

Foreword	*Cento Veljanovski*	5
The Author		8
I.		9
Are Markets Compatible with Socialist Ethics?		10
The Market: a Tool of Capitalism or Socialism		13
Is Market Socialism merely Social Democracy Dressed Up?		14
What Is Market Socialism?		15
'A Brick Wall of Self-contradiction'		17
'Social Ownership' Equals State Ownership		19
'The State-owned Market'?		20
II.		22
How Much 'Active Enforcement'?		23
Starting-Gates and End-States		25
Equal Opportunity: 'Fair' and 'Unfair' Advantages		27
The Confusion of Lotteries		28
A Positive-Sum Game		29
III.		31
'Building Socialism' via Markets?		32
'A Dull Mumbo-Jumbo'		33
Further Reading		36
Summary		Back cover

[3]

Foreword

THERE IS little doubt that the intellectual foundations of socialism lie in tatters. With the dramatic events of the last year in Eastern Europe the belief that socialism can improve the economic welfare of a nation, let alone that of its citizens, has been decisively shattered. Almost the entire Eastern bloc is moving towards markets and private property as the economies of these countries attempt to recover from the stultifying effect of central planning.

In the face of intellectual incoherence and economic failure, some cherish the desire to reconstruct socialism by advancing a new doctrine – market socialism. This is the attempt to combine the efficiency of markets with the traditional concerns of socialists for the common ownership of property and for egalitarianism. Anthony de Jasay's penetrating *Occasional Paper* punctures this attempt. He shows it to be based on woolly and self-contradictory arguments, and on an agenda which is logically little more than old-style socialism. The insurmountable hurdle for the advocates of market socialism is, according to Jasay, that it does not exist.

The deficiencies of the dislocated theorising of the intellectuals of market socialism rotate around the institutional and social dimensions of the proposed socialist market-place.

Consider the institutions which are responsible for a market's efficiency. A market is simply a form of social and economic organisation based on consensual voluntary exchanges. Markets exist in some form in all societies. If a state monopoly supplies a service which citizens can purchase, a market can be said to exist – people can either buy the service or not. But the efficiency of a market is the joint result of private property and of competition. The notion that one can have a market to allocate goods and services once they are produced whilst removing the incentives and penalties that would normally determine *how* they are produced and in what quantities is, to say the least, quaint, and in practice would inflict widespread inefficiency. Prices will no longer convey essential economic information to workers, producers, suppliers, and consumers; as a result, society's resources will not flow to their most valuable uses. But this, Jasay points out, is precisely what lies behind market socialism. Socialist markets are meant to operate in consumers' but not in producers' goods. In the productive sector capital would not be owned by individuals – it would be 'social property' owned by some undefined entity called society or the collective or the state. It is argued that if 'workers' or 'society' own capital and firms, the alleged inequities of capitalism would be avoided. As Jasay shows, whatever the rhetorical camouflage, social property ultimately is state ownership: in short, a productive sector in which property rights are not private, transferable and divisible. 'Social property' will neuter the market and make what is left impotent to engender the efficiency which is the objective of the New Left in seeking to harness the market to socialism.

The other crack in the intellectual foundations of market socialism is its policies for equality. Markets derive their efficiency from the fact that there are winners and losers, risk-takers and bankruptcies, entrepreneurs and uncertainty. The socialist ethic seeks to avoid losses and losers; to achieve more equal outcomes. However, such end-state egalitarianism jars with market forces. If the best that the successful producer or the hard worker can achieve is the wealth and status of the less-motivated members of society, there will be no point in above-average effort and ambition. In consequence, the wealth of society will dwindle.

Market socialism attempts to deal with these disincentive effects by invoking the notion of 'starting-gate equality' or, more simply, equality of opportunity. It supplies the reader with a vision of a world in which individuals start with equal wealth and with their natural advantages or disadvantages somehow compensated for. This is appealing. Why should the fool born into wealth and privilege have life-long advantages which the bright lad from the inner city has not? Obviously this is unfair. But to make it fair requires a powerful state with great power to create the identikit citizen. Life is not like a horse race where all participants gallop to a dead heat at the finishing line. People are born, educated, work, have families, grow old and die. One generation dovetails into the next; assets and debts are bequeathed to future generations. Starting-gate equality entails in practice a welfare state with large police and confiscatory powers. It is therefore *not* a possible substitute for 'end-state equality'.

If this reasoning is correct then the egalitarian aspects of market socialism destroy the alleged efficiency of its attempt to use markets. If 'equal opportunity' means that the gains from success, risk-taking, entrepreneurship and hard work are subject to expropriation by the state, the wealth-creating individual will lose his or her incentive to produce the wealth upon which the socialist's programme rests.

Anthony de Jasay's essay addresses these contradictions of current thinking about market socialism. The above summary does not do justice to the depth and wit of his analysis. As East and West move closer to market economies and seek to redefine socialism in terms not wholly dissimilar from those of capitalism, there is a danger that the vocabulary of the marketplace will be corrupted so that the same terms will mean something quite different in the political lexicon of vying groups. Anthony de Jasay cogently argues that 'market socialism' is a contradiction in terms. He has examined the case(s) put forward by a group of academics aimed at rebuilding the intellectual foundations of socialism. He believes that they have failed.

The Institute of Economic Affairs is an educational charity which does not express a corporate view. Mr de Jasay's *Occasional Paper* therefore contains his views alone and not those of the Institute. Nevertheless, the Institute offers this *Occasional Paper* as a contribution to an important debate in political economy.

March 1990   CENTO VELJANOVSKI

The Author

ANTHONY DE JASAY was born in Hungary in 1925, and has studied in Budapest, Perth (Western Australia), and Oxford. He left Hungary upon the change-over to the socialist régime in 1948. He was a Research Fellow in Economics at Nuffield College, Oxford from 1957-62. He then went into the finance and investment banking business in Paris, 1962-79. For the last ten years he has made his home in Normandy, where he now lives in semi-retirement.

His scholarly interests switched (in his own words, he has 'undergone a conversion') from economics to political philosophy, which has resulted in two books: *The State* (Oxford: Basil Blackwell, 1985); *Social Contract, Free Ride* (Oxford: Clarendon Press, 1989).

Market Socialism: A Scrutiny 'This Square Circle'
A. de JASAY

NEVER KICK a doctrine when it is down; the present is hardly the time to rub in the humiliations of socialism, in disarray as a political and economic theory and failed as a practice of government. This is not a rubbing-in essay. On the other hand, now is very much the season for attempts to reformulate, or as we have learnt to say, to 'restructure' socialism, openly defaulting on its heaviest liabilities, and taking it out of bankruptcy under some less tarnished identity. If only to protect the public, these attempts should be submitted to fairly beady-eyed scrutiny. The present, beady-eyed essay looks at the favourite candidate for such a new, post-bankruptcy identity.

In *Market Socialism*,[1] a team of Fabian social science teachers presents a collection of papers avowedly designed to rebuild an intellectually tenable position for the Left. The authors proceed partly by jettisoning some of the doctrinal baggage socialism has found too heavy to carry, partly by cross-breeding 'socialism' with 'market' to demonstrate that the union is both possible and desirable, and would have as its progeny a richer mix of efficiency and justice than any type of organisation that has yet been tried.

I

THERE IS A MINOR and a major move in this exit from bankruptcy's Chapter 11.[2] The minor move, which may serve as a hedge against

[1] Julian Le Grand and Saul Estrin (eds.), *Market Socialism*, Oxford: The Clarendon Press, 1989. Subsequent references to authors' papers in this collection are cited in brackets in my text, with page references where appropriate.
[2] Chapter 11 is a US form of corporate re-organisation which falls short of liquidation.

the major move not succeeding, consists in denying that the realisation of socialism entails recourse to *any* particular set of means (Estrin and Le Grand, p. 2). This must mean, conversely, that the employment of a particular set of means need not signify that it is socialism or anything like it that is being built; the means do not identify the end pursued. Hence if nationalisation, planning, regulation, price or rent control, queueing, sharply progressive taxation or a certain type of public education prove to be counterproductive in practice and untenable in theory, it should be easy for socialists to repudiate them without in any way abjuring socialism, for the former are merely contingent features of a possible socialist system; some other socialist system could do without them; and their presence neither qualifies a state of affairs or the thrust of policy as socialist, nor discredits socialism if they are condemned. This is a more refined echo of the perennial and unbeatable defence which makes all tangible evidence irrelevant by declaring about Soviet Russian experience that it did not discredit socialism because it was not socialist, but Stalinist and bureaucratic.

The authors of *Market Socialism*, quite astutely, generalise this defence: *no* objectionable feature of an existing system that calls itself socialist counts as evidence one way or the other. No empirically observable detail of its policies can serve as an argument that socialism is not a worthwhile goal. Thanks to this defence, socialism becomes a highly mobile and elusive target. Its definition is purged of falsifiable propositions. Such alternatives as 'the means of production are/are not privately owned', 'workers hire/are hired by capital', or 'access to food and shelter is/is not regulated by purchasing power' no longer necessarily distinguish a capitalist from a socialist society. It is only clear what socialism is *not* – no existing arrangement is – while what it *is* will be revealed only by the future, and then only if we have the good taste and judgement to embrace market socialism.

Are Markets Compatible with Socialist Ethics?

The question whether reliance on markets is compatible with the ethics of socialist man 'cannot be fully resolved until we have a working model' of market socialism (Miller, p. 48) – a test which does not threaten by its imminence. The internal contradictions of the Yugoslav system of worker ownership are no arguments against it, since 'as our understanding of co-operatives increases, we are [sic] able to devise alternative arrangements which preserve both enterprise-level democracy and economy-wide efficiency' (Estrin, p. 184) – though the profane reader wonders why, in that case, 40 years of experience did not enable the hapless Yugoslavs to have either democracy or efficiency, let alone both at the same time.

Dissociation of socialism from empirically falsifiable descriptive statements (e.g. 'in socialism, workers hire managers', or 'unearned income is taxed more heavily than earned', etc.) and indeed from all empirical precedents (e.g. 'Sweden' or 'Yugoslavia'), should protect it from positivist attacks, and ease the major move, the projection of a new identity. Its new name attractively couples the currently fashionable ('market') with the nostalgically retro ('socialism'). For this union really to work, however, it is necessary to dissolve another, that is, to 'decouple capitalism and markets' (Estrin and Le Grand, p. 2), for the two are wrongly yet strongly linked in the public mind.

There are, in fact, two links, one philosophical, the other historical. The philosophical link was first asserted by Mises[1] in 1920, for whom the information embodied in prices, necessary for efficiency in resource allocation, could be generated only by a competitive market. His argument was completed by Hayek[2] who added the essential element of a discovery process, developing and spreading otherwise unavailable, latent information, that is part of price formation by a multitude of economic agents.

The socialist counter-argument, that no logical links existed between capitalism and efficient pricing, set out in the 1930s by Lerner and Lange,[3] centred around the theoretical possibility of

---

[1] Ludwig von Mises, 'Die Wirtschaftsrechnung im sozialistischen Gemeinwesen', *Archiv fuer Sozialwissenschaften*, 1920, trans. as 'Economic Calculation in the Socialist Commonwealth', in F. A. Hayek (ed.), *Collectivist Economic Planning*, London: Routledge, 1935.

[2] F. A. Hayek in Hayek (ed.), *ibid.*

[3] A. P. Lerner, 'Economic Theory and Socialist Economy', *Review of Economic Studies*, 1934-35; Oskar Lange, 'On the Economic Theory of Socialism, I-II', *Review of Economic Studies*, October 1936 and February 1937.

finding market-clearing prices by simulating the responses capitalist producers would make to perceptible shortages and surpluses of exchangeable goods. This controversy, which went down in the history of economics as the 'Calculation Debate', in my view cannot be usefully pursued on a purely formal logical level.

On the substantive level, the key question to be settled is the reason adduced for expecting participants in a market to behave in a manner that will make the market an efficient instrument of resource allocation. In the context of the 'socialist market', this calls above all for settling the principal-agent problem. While it is present in both a real and a simulated market, there is good reason to hold that it works one way where property rights are private (i.e., attach to *individuals*), another way where they are collective (i.e., attach to *holistic entities* like the workforce, the commune, the state). The difference is fundamental, and suggests that managers of collectively owned, non-capitalist enterprises neither would nor could successfully simulate capitalist responses and reproduce the market processes and the resource transfers they induce. This argument is strongly supported both by the micro-economic theory of property rights and agency, and by the depressingly monotonous failure of repeated 'market-oriented' reforms in socialist economies – reforms that have always fought shy of reassigning ultimate, properly subdivided and clearly defined property rights to *persons*.

Even if these arguments were not conclusive and the issue were open, the onus would still be on socialists to show that, contrary to the record and to the state of the Calculation Debate, anything a capitalist market can do, the socialist one could do as well. No trace of meeting this obviously central requirement appears in *Market Socialism*, except for a bland and platitudinous reference to the calculation problem (Miller, pp. 30-31) as a reason for recourse to markets, rather than as a reason for questioning *whether* socialist markets, too, *can* 'calculate'. Why markets under socialism should be expected to achieve efficient allocation, or indeed to exist at all except as fakes – which is the sole really contentious issue in the Calculation Debate – is passed over in complete silence and incomprehension. Instead, we are airily told not to fret, because for reasons that are not revealed, 'in a socialist market economy . . . the makers of cheese will adjust their supply week by week to match the demand' (Miller, p. 38), and that is all there is to it. But it is not at all clear *why* they would adjust week by week, or ever, especially as doing so is neither always simple, nor convenient, nor costless. Simply to suppose that they would is begging a fairly basic question the authors may or may not have grasped, but have certainly not answered.

The Market: a Tool of Capitalism or Socialism

The historical link between capitalism and market, in turn, is not (*pace* Marx) a matter of historical necessity – the capitalist 'mode' entailing 'production for exchange', other 'modes' entailing 'production for needs'. It is merely a matter of historical coincidence that the abstract institution of the market, which is of course more than just the heir to the medieval fair, happened to evolve at the same time as, and in the frame of, the capitalist 'relations of production', though no doubt it could have evolved in other 'frames' as well. Apologists for capitalism usurp the market, appropriating it as if the market – an efficient institution – depended for its functioning on capitalism – a repugnant and alienating system. However, the suggestion that market and capitalism go together is but 'a sleight of hand' (Miller, p. 25). Traditional socialists fall for this trick, and think they dislike and mistrust markets when in fact it is capitalism they reject. This is a confusion (Miller, p. 29), a failure to see that the market can be trained to serve socialist goals just as it now serves capitalist ones. Indeed, though the authors do not say so, they tacitly treat the market as a neutral tool in the hands of its political master who can use it in fashioning the kind of society he wants. Gone, then, is the characterisation of capitalism as a design for the pursuit of profit, socialism as one for the satisfaction of 'needs' – as is the clear distinction between obedience to impersonal market forces under capitalism, to conscious social choice under socialism. We can, in sum, have the best of both at one and the same time.

For market socialism is nothing if not pragmatic. Markets

appear to be good for some purposes in some areas, planning is good for other purposes in other areas, and there is no apprehension that the two may not mix admirably well. Worker co-operatives 'may not be optimal for all industries at all times' (Miller, p. 36), but then they surely must be for some industries at certain times. '[I]t is not clear that one would want to rule out capitalist acts between consenting adults altogether' (Estrin and Le Grand, p. 15, Winter, p. 154). '[G]overnment could seek to make the market responsive to social goals such as greater social justice, equality and full employment' (Plant, p. 52). '[C]entral planning of an entire economy is unfeasible' (Estrin and Le Grand, p. 11), but one must choose the right balance between market and planning, and indicative planning is valuable, notably as a 'guide to medium-term economic development in the medium term [sic]' (ibid.). Above all, market socialists can safely count on the market for delivering material welfare, yet need not condone the unjust, 'morally arbitrary' way it distributes it. Only social democracy, untroubled by principles and systemic clashes, is as confident of having its cake and eating it as market socialism.

Is Market Socialism merely Social Democracy Dressed Up?

Does this self-assured eclecticism in fact mean that market socialism is nothing else but re-packaged social democracy, with at its base an economy capitalist enough to work, and capable of holding up a strongly interventionist and redistributive super-structure, pushing union power, regulation, egalitarianism and welfarism, but only to the point beyond which adverse economic and social trade-offs become unaffordable, and never quite going over the brink? The answer appears to be 'no', for reasons that are not wholly clear and turn out to be surprising when they are elucidated. The main point seems to be that, unlike social democracy, market socialism will do more than merely *redress* capitalist outcomes; it will *do away with* the institutions chiefly responsible for these outcomes – and first of all with the main culprit, the limited liability company (Winter, p. 140). The latter is noxious because it facilitates private concentrations of power outside government control (a tendency which, if true, would surely be a contribution to the preservation of individual freedom by virtue of the counterweights it provided against the omnipotence of the state), but also because it separates ownership and control, and therefore – whatever the modern theory of the firm may say – it cannot be 'relied upon to produce efficient results'; on the other hand,

> '[b]oth the inefficiencies and the abuse of economic power can be reduced, if not eliminated, by placing both ownership and control in the hands of the entire work-force'. (Winter, p. 142.)

It is hard to take this sort of statement seriously but one must try. Market socialists ought to be especially aware of what markets are suited to do. The separation of management control from ownership, while admittedly a possible source of inefficiency, is broadly taken care of by the market for corporate control or, in plainer English, by the threat of the take-over bid. The more open and free is that particular market, the less the likelihood of inefficiency due to the principal-agent problem. The owner-manager, who has total security of managerial tenure, is potentially more inefficient than the professionally run corporation, since he is much freer not to 'maximise', and can indulge his fancies – as the history of so many family-owned firms and of capricious robber barons demonstrates. Unfortunately for the market socialist thesis, however, worker co-operatives are *a priori* worse than either, their weird and hybrid incentive structure pushing them to choose 'socially' wrong, inefficient factor proportions and a sub-optimal scale. The authors of *Market Socialism* appear to be aware of this (Abell, p. 98, Estrin, pp. 175-76, 183), yet they let stand the bizarre juxtaposition of capitalist inefficiency/co-operative efficiency. For the structural deformities of the latter, they propose truly lame remedies that might or might not work if they were tried but, perhaps fortunately for the market socialist argument, have not been, and the fact that they have not been is surely significant.

What Is Market Socialism?

If one is to believe the disclaimer that market socialism is not social democracy (Estrin and Le Grand, p. 13), nor the putting into practice of any particular set of reputedly socialist policies (Estrin and Le Grand, p. 2), what exactly is it? The answers, such as they are, have to be found by exegesis, for the authors do not tempt Nemesis by setting them out in the shape of a clearly visible target. We do know, however, that it is a system where, contrary to socialism proper, decisions to allocate resources are taken in response to price signals emitted by market mechanisms. But why are these signals heeded? Innocently, the book takes it for granted that, quite simply, they are, '[s]ince market producers are generally motivated by profit' (Estrin and Le Grand, p. 3). However, it is clear on reflection (and the hurt surprise of socialist countries that tried to abandon the command economy without also re-defining and de-centralising property rights and found themselves with an economy that heeded no signals of any sort, shows it conclusively) that this is by no means 'generally' the case. It will be the case only if property rights are private in the sense that whoever is entitled to allocate certain resources is also entitled fully to profit from good allocations and is made to suffer from bad ones – either directly if he is the owner, or through some control mechanism if he is a manager. In the latter case tricky problems may start to arise, which, however, are as nothing to the problem to be faced when the manager is not the agent of the owner, but the simulated agent of a holistic pseudo-owner.

So far, however, market socialism looks not too unlike a kind of capitalism in discreet incognito. Yet as one looks closer, troubles of identity emerge. Consumer goods are permitted to be privately owned by firms (which, in turn, may or may not be privately owned) and by individuals but only within the limits imposed on the wealth and income of the latter by the requirements of equality. Subject to these limits, they can be bought and sold; at least one necessary condition of a market for consumer goods is thus fulfilled. Ownership of producer goods, and of their assemblies, however, is subject to more stringent restraints, which react back on consumer goods and negate other necessary conditions of a market for the latter.

'Provided that the capitalist acquired the productive assets legitimately, and here *I would rule out inheritance*' (Winter, p. 154, my italics), puts narrow bounds on the permissible size of asset holdings, for since the market must not permanently reward one participant more than another, and incomes after tax are to be broadly equal, the capitalist, barred from *inheriting*, cannot *accumulate* from his profits either. The size of a privately owned firm, moreover, is to be decided at the discretion of its employees:

> 'An attractive solution [sic] to the problem of how large a company should be before it ceases to be privately owned is to allow the workforce to make the choice.' (Winter, p. 157.)

What is more devastating, and indeed startling in the context of a proposal to rely on markets, is that 'private ownership is tolerated so long as the owners do not wish to sell their assets' (Winter, p. 162). The ban on negotiability, reinforced by the ban on joint-stock limited liability, would put paid, in the name of market socialism, to any chance of having a market for producer goods, and assets as claims on producer goods or on income streams. The question then arises as to how a market for consumer goods alone can function efficiently or at all, if there can be, for practical purposes, no market in the resources that it takes to make consumer goods.

'A Brick Wall of Self-contradiction'

It really seems that market socialism has, at this point if not before, run into a brick wall of total self-contradiction. Does it have some clever way around it, by inventing a species of property rights which permits exchanges on *all* markets, and permits market disequilibria to result in profits for those who best read market signals and thus do most to eliminate the disequilibria? Can it, in other words, devise a hitherto untried type of ownership that would be private in its effect on people's motivations, yet non-private in that it would not reproduce capitalist domination, capitalist inequality, capitalist 'moral arbitrariness'? Miller declares, as if this were obvious once you thought of it, that '[i]t is quite possible to be for markets and against capitalism' (Miller, p. 25). Yet the possibility is remote, and certainly not evident. It depends on the discovery of this new institution of 'both-private-and-not-private' ownership – an attempt whose success has yet to be demonstrated.

As we shall see, if the theoretical attempt can be made, let alone made successfully, it calls for mental contortions of greater improbability than market socialists seem to realise. They appear to think – and if they do not, they unwittingly convey – that property rights which have both these attributes at the same time, are inherent and can be discovered in what they choose to call 'social ownership'. Once again, the meaning of the term is hidden in verbiage, and is rendered positively enigmatic by assertions that it does not mean what the lay reader would think it meant. It is *not* state ownership: if it were, nationalisation would be an identifying characteristic of the building of market socialism, and we have been explicitly told that it is not. The authors of *Market Socialism* profess to think little of it as a policy. Is, then, 'social ownership' ownership by the workers? Again the answer is 'no'. Communal ownership is potentially market-socialist if it concerns a mere island 'in a hostile capitalist environment' (Estrin, p. 185) but becomes 'workers' capitalism, not socialism' (*ibid.*) if it is the prevalent form of ownership, since each commune would be motivated to act selfishly with respect to society as a whole. The plot thickens, the puzzle gets ever more insoluble. Market socialist property rights 'preclude any direct ownership or control by workers. . . . Ownership of co-operatives . . . must therefore be *social*' (*ibid.*, my italics). Under social ownership, 'the capital stock is owned collectively by society, and is merely administered by particular groups of workers' (Estrin, p. 173).

Who, however, *is* society? Is it not the entity represented by the supreme proxyholder, the state? How can ownership be vested in 'society' without the ownership rights being exercised by the state? If the owner is not any of its subsets (a municipality, a co-operative, a commune of kindred spirits, or whatever), but really society 'as a whole', social ownership is *ipso facto* state ownership, social owner-decisions are government decisions (however unsatisfactory a proxy the government may be for society, there is no other above it), and no linguistic figleaves will alter these identities by one iota. The state, then, owns the capital stock, and 'democratically run' groups of workers 'administer' but do not 'control' it. The reader who thought that elsewhere in this 'reconstruction of the intellectual base of the Left' he saw market socialism held up as a superior *alternative* to nationalisation, must be rubbing his eyes.

'Social Ownership' Equals State Ownership

'Social ownership', if it means anything at all beyond chatter, is clearly state ownership, for only the latter satisfies the apparent requirements of neutralising the owner's selfishness *vis-à-vis* society; it is only society as such that has no 'particular will' in conflict with the 'general will'. Yet it is not certain that market socialists realise that it is state ownership they are calling for. Only sundry *obiter dicta* suggest that in a vague way they do. One of them describes the passage to market socialism thus:

> '... the state would transform all publicly and privately held equity into debenture stock, upon which the (self managed) firms would have to pay the going interest rate. At the same time, the authorities would create a number of new holding companies, to each of which would be entrusted certain assets in the national portfolio. Since the state has the task of creating the holding companies, *it might choose to retain ownership* itself ...' (Estrin, p. 192, my italics.)

But does market socialism leave it any other choice? It must not hand back the equity in the 'national portfolio' to the citizenry at large, for that would in no time recreate capitalist institutions and capitalist outcomes; then market socialism would have to be introduced all over again. Nor must it hand it over to firms, letting them be not only 'self-managed' but also 'self-owned', for this would be taking a wrong turning, leading to workers' capitalism. The state, in sum, not only 'might choose' to be the universal owner, but *must* do so unless market socialism is to degenerate into mere social democracy. A good deal of perhaps unconscious camouflage, in the shape of state holding companies acting as competing venture capitalists, and so forth, is going on in the book to avoid having to face state ownership openly. The words 'social ownership' are the recurrent motif in this camouflage. It is no more a genuinely new type of ownership, holding out the stimuli of private rights without their propensity to reproduce capitalism, than market socialism is a genuine doctrine.

If taking capital into state ownership is mandatory – for any alternative would negate essential market socialist postulates – market socialism is no longer a moving target. We find that, perhaps unbeknown to its inventors, it has been nailed down, committed to at least one 'particular means', nationalisation, if it really seeks to realise its avowed ends. Can market socialists live with this? Perhaps understandably in view of the dilemma, they choose not to say.

An ironic consequence of their implicit commitment is that, even if other self-imposed constraints did not confine the 'market' of market socialism to consumer goods alone, 'social ownership' of productive assets would. Genuine market exchanges presuppose among other things a plurality of principals owning goods to be exchanged, and having dissimilar preferences or expectations. When the state is the sole owner of the assets to be exchanged, it can at best organise exchanges between its right hand and its left hand, getting up a 'simulated market' generating simulated asset prices, a simulated 'going' interest rate, simulated gains and losses of simulated efficiency and, at the end of the road, simulated shops pretending to sell simulated goods.

'The State-owned Market'?

Undaunted, market socialists will have both state ownership and market, and introduce a near-perfect oxymoron, the state-owned market:

> 'Under a scheme of this sort, the internal structure of productive enterprises would remain largely unchanged' [thanks for small mercies!] 'although of course their system of control would alter. However, an entirely new *state-owned capital market* would have to be created' (Estrin, p. 192, my italics).

What these words can possibly mean, and how such a market could be 'created', are details that remain unrevealed due perhaps to modesty, perhaps to the author's belief that a 'state-owned capital market' is self-explanatory in the same way as 'state-owned steelworks' or (in what is probably the crowning example of self-explanation) Engels's 'state-owned brothels'.

Other contributors commit themselves even less in the matter of how real markets in non-capitalist property rights are to arise. In characteristically pragmatic spirit, it is suggested that all manner of arrangements could be envisaged, ranging from various types of co-operatives to 'labour-capital partnerships' (Abell, pp. 95, 98), excluding only the joint-stock company. Labour-capital partnerships differ both from capitalist enterprises and from pure co-operatives; in fact, they appear to embody the vices and virtues of both in a diluted form. They look like the corporatist fudge, much tried by British governments of both parties since the Second World War, that may be the least unacceptable short-run *modus vivendi* for producer interests, but regularly ends up in the worst of both worlds for producers and consumers alike.

Fudged or clear-cut, non-private ownership is a core requirement of market socialism, and genuine markets must somehow prove to be compatible with it. It is the pivotal place of this condition that really differentiates market socialism from the bankrupt doctrine of orthodox and, as I would insist, genuine socialism, as well as from the *ad hoc* compromises of social democracy. Market socialism, in order to rid itself of the crushing liabilities of genuine socialism while still making good its claim to being more than just the boring old welfare state, must invent something desperately original by way of what property rights should entail and in whom they should be vested. It is dismaying to find, then, that the particular author whose lot it was to go beyond airy anti-private generalities and to spell out these matters, is not familiar with the meaning of ownership and has not mastered the distinction between creditor and owner, debt and equity, interest and profit. In the same breath he (probably rightly) condemns workers' capitalism and communal ownership, prescribes the vesting of productive capital in 'society as a whole', yet assigns to the labour force of each enterprise 'one element of the entrepreneurial function: the right to the residual surpluses (profit from trading after all inputs have been paid for)' (Estrin, p. 186), the right in question being none other than equity ownership.

Manifestly, then, it is not 'productive capital' as such, but only some kind of gigantic prior charge on it, that is to be 'socially owned' by the state. The equity of each enterprise is to belong to workers' collectives (always provided that they do not buy or sell it or parts in it – a condition that is sure to give rise to lively and efficient asset markets). Back we go, then, to 'each of these groups of workers acting selfishly with respect to the broader society' (Estrin, p. 185), which was the reason for prescribing state, instead of group, ownership in the first place. At this point, one abandons vain exegesis; the more one looks to see how the circle could be squared, the rounder it stays.

II

MARKET SOCIALISTS ARE on intellectually less unfamiliar ground when, instead of dealing with such contrivances as equity, debt, market and profit, they turn to the final values – equality, freedom, distributive justice, the satisfaction of needs – that they expect the market as an instrument, allied to some ingenious if not wholly comprehensible reform of property rights, to procure. Arguing for these values and about ways to reach them has always been congenial to socialist thought (though more to its Proudhonian than its Marxist strain), in contrast to the value-neutral tendencies of liberalism. In addition, Plant and Abell, the authors whose contributions particularly address these issues, happen to reason better and less glibly than the others, and deserve more serious attention.

For genuine socialists, the notion of freedom conveys above all mankind winning mastery over matter, liberating itself from the tyranny of things, the blind caprice of 'reified relations'. It is a notion that alludes to scientific progress and political revolution, and whose subject is a collective, holistic one. Its bearing on individual choice is at best derivative and contingent; at worst, it dismisses choice as a selfish indulgence. Market socialists, by contrast, associate freedom primarily with individual choice in the classical liberal manner, and are pleased to note that the market is the economic institution *par excellence* that responds to preferences, just as democracy is the political institution *par excellence* that does so, though each weighs the preferences of different individuals in a particular manner. The democratic weighting – one man, one vote – is always egalitarian, the market weighting may be grossly inegalitarian if one man can back his preference with more money than another. It is for socialist policies to see to it that grossly unequal weights disappear. Various means can be employed to this end. Whatever they are, they are prefaced by a blanket dismissal of the costs and pains of applying them, and of the feedbacks leading back to the market economy:

> 'Nor is there any reason why a market socialist economy should not operate effectively in the presence of an active enforcement of such policies' (Estrin and Le Grand, p. 22).

Perhaps there isn't, but how do they know? – and how do *we*? Gratuitous assertions such as this one, only just acceptable in a party policy statement but not in an argument addressed to intellectuals, are not helpful for the declared aim of rebuilding 'the lost intellectual base' of the Left and 'its philosophical and economic foundations' (Preface, p. v).

How Much 'Active Enforcement'?

A good deal of 'active enforcement' would be required to establish 'market democracy', and more than we should at first think to secure freedom of choice, for the latter is not simply what it says. It is more than the non-imposition of any particular alternative out of a given set of them – what has unfortunately come to be called 'negative freedom'. It is also their availability, according to Miller, as 'real' rather than merely 'formal' options. On inspection, a formal option is one that is not one, while a choice is said to need resources before it can be acted upon. It would be better English not to call them 'options' when they are unreal, nor 'choices' when they cannot be acted upon, but the inept language about unreal options and impossible choices helps to slip in the similarly muddled notion of 'positive freedom'. As Miller clumsily puts it,

> 'freedom can be diminished not merely by legal prohibitions but also

by economic policies that deprive people of the material means *to act on their choices*' (Miller, p. 32, my italics).

More lucidly, and without talking of *choices* when he means *desires*, to shape one's life means 'to have abilities, resources and opportunities – that is to say, some command over resources', and cannot be separated from 'the capacity for agency and its associated resources' (Plant, p. 65). In the terminology of economics, negative freedom is the unobstructed faculty to take any option that falls *within* the individual's given budget of time, money and knowledge, while positive freedom has to do with widening the budget constraint. Having more positive freedom is a code word for having more wealth, more leisure, more knowledge – in sum, a richer life. But then why not *say* so? – why have recourse to the special code? For are not wealth, knowledge or leisure less emotion-laden words, and have they not a more settled and precise meaning, than freedom? Or is that precisely why market socialists, and others, draw them under the umbrella term of 'freedom' instead? They plead that 'it would be perverse' to regard 'a wealthy genius and a poor illiterate, both living under the rule of the same liberal law, as equally free' (Abell, p. 84). Users of the 'negative' freedom concept would have no inhibitions so to regard them; they could increase the information content of the comparison by adding that while both were 'equally' free, one was richer and cleverer than the other. This would tell us substantially more than the cryptic socialist statement that one had more 'positive' freedom than the other.

One suspects, however, that the call to give 'equal freedom' to all gets a wider and more favourable hearing than the seemingly far stronger demand to equalise everybody's wealth, leisure and knowledge. Hence packaging the latter demand under the bland name of 'positive freedom' masks the sting of a very demanding egalitarian norm. Indeed, when postulating that equality is a value in its own right, it is explicitly the equality of 'positive and negative freedoms' that is being stipulated (Abell, p. 80), for defined as they are, their equality will *ipso facto* give socialists all the equality of wealth, income, education and status that they are likely to want.

They want a good deal, but it is never finally clear just how much, for despite a few defiant assurances that we can safely afford social justice, since the market will go on delivering much the same riches regardless of how 'society' decides to distribute them, several contributors to the volume have some gut awareness that redistribution of the rewards market participants hand to each other must have some effect on the performance of the market economy; the goose will hardly remain forever indifferent to what happens to her golden eggs. Plant warns, pertinently, that '[i]f people know in advance that there will be equality of result however they act in the market, this will be a recipe for inefficiency' (p. 72) – to put it no higher. Since they could not be fooled for long, and *would* know in advance if there *were* to be equality of result, presumably there *must not be* equality of result – or so one would surmise, although as we shall see presently, one would be wrong.

Starting-Gates and End-States

Unease about the goose may have a small part in shaping the sort of equality market socialists are calling for, philosophical differences with genuine socialists a greater one. In the trendy words that have come to pollute the stagnant pool of political philosophy, they do not wish distribution to be governed solely or even mainly by 'patterned' or 'end-state' principles, but want distributive justice to emerge from just 'process' – their great remaining difference with liberals being that, for market socialists, just process yields acceptable end-state outcomes only if it begins at a specially designed 'starting-gate' of equal opportunity. Provided, however, that in socialism *starting-gates themselves are 'patterned'* as they should be, the outcomes of market processes will call for relatively little further state intervention to make the right, egalitarian end-state principle prevail – for it will then to a large extent prevail, as it were, of its own accord, assisted by the invisible hand.

This, then, is the great promise of equality of opportunity, the species of equality that offends least and is easiest to get past a somnolent moral consensus; for while there is no single end-state principle of equality that would not offend some strong moral intuition, some material interest, or both, equality of opportunity is at first sight soothing and almost wholly unexceptionable. Its appeal to our sense of justice (or, more insidiously, to our sense of 'fairness') is as broad as it is weak, while any vague threat it may represent to our vested interests looks tolerably easy to live with.

Proponents of the idea convey this impression (and, I dare say, convince themselves of it, too) by employing a particular paradigmatic imagery. Participation in the market economy is a trip, or a race. It has an 'entry point' or 'starting-gate', and a finishing line where prizes await the runners who win them in order of arrival. The winners get larger prizes than the others, but this inequality is a legitimate outcome of the process of matching the runners on a level track, provided the winners had no 'unfair' advantage, nor the losers a handicap, 'at the starting-gate'. Calling advantages that have helped winners to win *'unfair'*, and that we only recognise as such because their possessors have won, is of course vacuous in itself unless it gets content from a prior delineation between fair and unfair advantages. All market socialists would put greater wealth, a better education, a more extensive and highly placed network of friends and protectors on the wrong side of the dividing line. Many would hesitate about more brains, rare gifts, better looks, greater sex appeal. Most of them would not (though those who took the 'moral arbitrariness' of natural endowments seriously would clearly have to) classify greater industry, hard work, relentless application as unfair advantages, because they are owed to character, innate guts and strength of will that are, in turn, unearned. Great perplexity would surround the fairness or otherwise of sheer luck, which is the residual cause of differential performance after all other, specially identified advantages have been accounted for.

Evidently, if all differential performance on a level track is attributable to some advantage, whether innate or acquired, and if *all* advantages at the starting-gate are unfair, the only fair outcome of the race is all-round dead-heat – that is, 'equality of outcome'. Dead-heat is engineered by stripping the contestants at the starting-gate of their *alienable* advantages, such as wealth, or redistributing them until all possess them in equal measure, while compensating for *inalienable* advantages by a system of head starts and handicaps (positive and negative discriminations). However, racing history suggests that perfect handicapping is probably impossible, for residual advantages always manage to subsist. Nor would market socialists really want it, most being content to allow desert in some sense to earn differential rewards (Miller, p. 44), and believing that they can tell rewards due to some kind of desert from rewards due to unfair advantages.

Equal Opportunity: 'Fair' and 'Unfair' Advantages

In sum, under equal opportunity people retain some 'fair' advantages at the starting-gate to make the race interesting, but the rest of their advantages, inherited or acquired, are unfair and must be evened out one way or another. Lest we should think that, once that is done, the rest is really up to the individual contestants, it turns out that the end-state resulting at the finishing line, albeit a product of pure procedural justice, will still require adjustment guided by 'a theory of distributive justice, equality and community' (Plant, p. 76), which cannot 'be achieved without a powerful state' (*ibid.*, p. 77). Nevertheless, 'starting-gate redistribution' will have done much that would otherwise fall to 'end-state redistribution' to achieve, and this will bring to life a remarkable hybrid, 'market-oriented' in that it permits random outcomes, and socialist in that it does not.

The prize formulation of this clever synthesis is once again contributed by Miller:

> 'the system might have some of the features of a genuine lottery in which punters win on some rounds and lose on others, the net effect being relatively insignificant ... the socialist objection is ... to the kind of luck which, once enjoyed, puts its beneficiary into a position of permanent advantage' (Miller, p. 45).

Now winning on the lottery *is* a permanent advantage, unless there is a specific, built-in provision to *undo* it, ensuring by some means that the winner loses it again without undue delay. For instance, a combination of poor odds and an obligation to go on playing as long as he is ahead, would suffice to make him rapidly lose again the advantages he has won. Failing such a combination of adverse odds and obligation to play on, he could either take the money home, or profitably use it to buy more tickets for the next round of the lottery, since a sufficient proportion of tickets would be winning ones. At the odds offered by the 'lottery' of a market economy – that is, where the return on the average investment is better than zero – an initial advantage has a better than even chance of becoming cumulative, as each round is more likely to add to than subtract from the player's winnings.

But market socialism works by a different logic. It insists that the market shall be a *'genuine* lottery', not a game of *'cumulative* advantage' (Miller, p. 45, my italics).

The Confusion of Lotteries

The confusion about lotteries is not a pardonable slip of language or logic, for it leads to a gross confusion of the whole issue of equal opportunity in a market economy. A lottery is genuine if the distribution of all (positive and negative) prizes among the tickets is *random*. Miller appears to believe, however, that it is genuine only if the sum of the prizes is *zero* – a very different condition. This is nonsense, for the concept of lottery implies no particular sum, positive or negative. A more insidious fallacy is then committed in applying the false concept of lottery as a possible norm for the market. It is possible to hold that the distribution of prizes in the market is random. To stipulate that they have a zero sum is, on the contrary, to require an absurdity which contradicts the essential, *wealth-creating nature* of the market without which it would lose its whole point and would not exist. Gains and losses cannot possibly cancel out either interpersonally or intertemporally, but must be greater than zero both over all the players and over time as long as prizes breed more prizes – that is, in an economy where the productivity of capital (or, less metaphysically, the interest rate) is positive.

There seems to be a more than somewhat Freudian reason why a market socialist equates a properly ordered socialist market economy to a non-positive-sum game: for only in a world where no gain is permanent, let alone cumulative, can equal opportunity make sense as an identifiable end capable of being told apart from equality of results or 'end-states'. The slip of logic about lotteries reveals the self-destructive nature of the starting-gate 'paradigm'.

Suppose, first, that on the advent of market socialism an equal-opportunity placing of the contestants at the 'entry point' has been accomplished by appropriate juggling with endowments, advantages, handicaps, discriminations, and head starts. The starting-gate is thus properly 'patterned' and they now run the race. Anything they win is an advantage in the next race. However, since it is, by special stipulation, a 'genuine lottery' excluding permanent and, *a fortiori*, cumulative advantage, either no one wins, or all win the same prize, or if one wins a bigger prize, he hastens to play double or quits and quickly loses it. Thus when they are past the finishing line, no one has an advantage, let alone a permanent and still less a cumulative one. Happily, therefore, the finishing line of the first race proves to be the right, correctly 'patterned' starting-gate for the second race. The contestants again run it from an equal-opportunity position, presumably with the same result as the first race. So they can go on for any number of races. The equal-opportunity entry point, where each contestant is let loose on an even track, ensures that each finishing line is also a new entry-point of the same kind as the old. Each end-state faithfully reproduces the initial equal-opportunity position, and the just procedure duly generates a just outcome.

A Positive-Sum Game

Suppose next that the market economy is a positive-sum game. Gains and losses of a given participant do not tend to cancel out over time and, by the nature of market exchanges and the law of compound interest, the prizes of various kinds – differential earnings, profits, acquired skills, knowledge, goodwill – help win additional prizes. The contestants are again lined up at the 'entry point' so as to enjoy equal opportunity. Now, however, any advantage is retained and becomes the source of further advantage. Whoever discovers marketable knowledge can accumulate capital, whoever gets hold of capital finds it easier to acquire knowledge, and so on in a cumulative process of 'positive-sum' exchanges. Under such conditions, the 'finishing line' of any one race will no longer serve as an equal-opportunity starting-gate for the following race. For each race, contest or round, an equal-opportunity starting-gate has to be deliberately constructed all over again by stripping people of their acquired advantages, evening out differentials, arranging handicaps, awarding head starts, and so forth. Unhappily, and in contrast to the first scenario, this means that at each finishing line at the latest, distributive justice has to be administered to the participants before they are off again to the next round, according to 'patterned' principles, to preserve a particular end-state of no net advantages at the new starting-gate. Aiming at equal opportunity *means* aiming *at an end-state* of which it happens to be a characteristic feature, that is, *where no one is ahead.*

If such is the case, however, one might as well not bother about equality of opportunity, for it turns out to be both analytically and operationally indistinguishable from equality of outcomes, and collapses into the latter.

The truth of the matter, of course, is that Ronald Dworkin's catchy, media-friendly metaphor of the 'starting-gate' trips him up, and with him many of the lesser lights of the soft Left. If the world began at some starting-gate where the representative economic agent got going and ended some distance away at a finishing line where he had to stop, equal opportunity at the starting-gate might be a meaningful condition, independent of outcomes. It would be consistent with unequal outcomes at the finishing line, and would be operationally different from equality of end-states, for starting-gate and finishing line would be in two different places. But if the world continued beyond the putative finishing line, and the race went on or a new one began, the absurd zero-sum 'genuine lottery' requirement would have to be satisfied for starting-gate equal opportunity to be preserved.

However, since there is no Day One and each starting-gate is the finishing line of the preceding round, while each finishing line is the starting-gate of the next one, we are dealing with an infinite regress of 'races' or 'lotteries'. At the finish of each race, the participants are further removed from equal opportunity than at its start. People have parents who have transmitted advantages to them; they pursue careers, save money, win friends, and in turn transmit some of these advantages to their children. How often during a race, or after how many races, is equal opportunity to be restored by equalising end-states? Can we leave it to a revolution or a lost war every thirty years or so? The sole logical market socialist answer, of course, is that to secure equal opportunity, we have to keep removing advantages all the time *as they accrue*, while confidently expecting that people will keep on accumulating them. We are invited to believe that they will not get wise to the fact that a 'patterned' end-state principle is being busily applied to their income, wealth, education or anything else that helps them win 'races' or 'lotteries', and makes for a competitive economy.

If we abandon the fiction of discrete rounds of finite length, and are facing a continuum of competitive economic activity instead, the distinction between equal opportunities and equal outcomes loses all meaning. Goodbye, then, to equal opportunity as an intelligible and at least metaphorically plausible policy goal; welcome to equal opportunity as an inoffensive and reassuring form of words that market socialists (and others) can use when they mean equal end-states or plain equality. Vain as it may be, one can nonetheless express the wish that people in general, would-be political philosophers in particular, would learn to say what they mean.

III

BY PROTESTING TOO MUCH, and promising too much, blueprints of social organisation have tended to discredit themselves and their draughtsmen. Genuine socialism used to promise material progress, equality, and freedom conceived as the end of alienation and subjection to blind economic mechanisms. It is of course true that it never fulfilled any of these promises, let alone all three, and that it could never have done so even if its earthly incarnations had not all been dogged by bad luck in the geographical and historical 'parameters' that fell to their lot. I would nevertheless argue that had it offered a trade-off of *more of two* desirable ends in exchange for *less of a third*, it might have earned a degree of recognition for honesty. At least its ultimate loss of credibility might have been less total. Striving for material progress, expecting ever greater hordes of machines served by 'work collectives' of progressively more mis-motivated men to generate abundance from misdirected resources, was a forlorn hope. Without the fatal ambition to grow as rich and have as clever gadgets as capitalism, the socialist state might have come a little closer to redeeming its promises of equality and liberation, for at least at first sight these two are not mutually exclusive objectives in a simple, quasi-pastoral economy stretched by no exacting demands.

Alternatively, the blueprint might have offered to the socialist élite a strictly non-market, state capitalist system with an avowedly inegalitarian command economy running on quasi-slave labour; such a version of socialism might make material progress of sorts, while also living up to some albeit contorted ideal of liberation from the alienating relations of 'production for exchange'. It would of course have to shut out, together with equality, all temptation of self-determination and all basis for personal autonomy, and firmly refuse to seek popularity by compromise; with these provisos, however, it could prove to be as credible an undertaking as it was unlovely. The *triple* promise of welfare, liberty and equality, however, is too much and has so far always proved to be so, condemning all three to shameful defaults.

One could no doubt find *a priori* reasons why this could not have turned out otherwise, but in the face of the empirical evidence, that effort is hardly worth the trouble. Whether a less foolhardy or less insincere blueprint, promising a measure of equality and relative freedom from the compulsions of the market in a slack economic backwater, would have called forth more trust and tolerance, can of course only be guessed at, but the intellectual and moral fiasco would have been less humiliating.

'Building Socialism' via Markets?

Market socialism, for all its contrary protestations, shows every sign of setting out to march in genuine socialism's footsteps.

IEA PUBLICATIONS
Subscription Service

An annual subscription is the most convenient way to obtain our publications. Every title we produce in all our regular series will be sent to you immediately on publication and without further charge, representing a substantial saving.

Individual subscription rates*

Britain: £30·00 p.a. including postage.
£28·00 p.a. if paid by Banker's Order.
£18·00 p.a. to teachers and students who pay *personally*.

Europe: £30·00 p.a. including postage.

South America: £40·00 p.a. or equivalent.

Other Countries: Rates on application. In most countries subscriptions are handled by local agents. Addresses are available from the IEA.

* These rates are *not* available to companies or to institutions.

To: The Treasurer, Institute of Economic Affairs,
2 Lord North Street, Westminster,
London SW1P 3LB

I should like to subscribe from ....

I enclose a cheque/postal order for:

☐ £30·00

☐ £18·00   I am a teacher/student at ....

....

☐ Please send a Banker's Order form.

☐ Please send an invoice.

☐ Please charge my credit card:

Please tick ☐ VISA ☐ Access ☐ AMERICAN EXPRESS ☐ ◐

Card No: [   ]

In addition I would like to purchase the following previously published titles:

....

....

Name ....

Address ....   } BLOCK LETTERS PLEASE

....

.... Post Code ....

Signed .... Date ....

OP84/2

OP84/2

The names

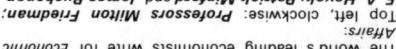

The world's leading economists write for *Economic Affairs*:
Top left, clockwise: Professors *Milton Friedman; F. A. Hayek; Patrick Minford* and *James Buchanan*.

Editor: Robert Miller

Editorial Consultant: Arthur Seldon CBE

Published bi-monthly in association with The Institute of Economic Affairs by City Publications Ltd.

Economic Affairs is the only magazine to offer an international platform for market economists — and their critics — analysing current or impending events and trends in political economy. Each issue has a major theme devoted to a subject of topical interest. Essential reading for economists, students, businessmen, politicians, teachers — and everyone interested in economic affairs.

SUBSCRIBE TODAY!

* delete where inapplicable

Please send me _____ copies of ECONOMIC AFFAIRS for one year (five issues)

I enclose my cheque/P.O. for £/$* _____ (Cheques payable to 'Economic Affairs.')

NAME _____ (Block Capitals)

POSITION _____ (If Applicable)

INSTITUTION _____ (If Applicable)

ADDRESS (Home/Institution) _____

POST CODE _____

☐ Please charge my credit card: £/$*_____

Signature _____

Please tick ☐ VISA ☐ Access ☐ American Express

Date _____ Card No. _____

Please tick where relevant
☐ This is a RENEWAL.   ☐ I would like information on the IEA's PUBLICATIONS/ SUBSCRIPTION SERVICE
☐ This is a NEW SUBSCRIPTION

SEND PAYMENT TO: Economic Affairs, Magazine Subscription Dept., FREEPOST, Luton, LU1 5BR, UK.

The faces

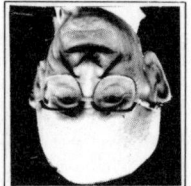
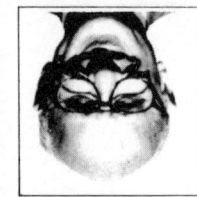
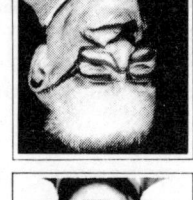

The magazine

RATES

INDIVIDUAL:
☐ UK & Europe £18.00
☐ Outside Europe $54.00

INSTITUTION:
☐ UK & Europe £33.00
☐ Outside Europe $78.00

STUDENT:
☐ UK & Europe £15.00
☐ Outside Europe $36.00

☐ Please invoice me/my organisation*

NB: Individual rate applies to educational establishments

☏ **Telephone 0582-32640 with your credit card details**

Despite an occasional doubt, an *ad hoc* disclaimer, a shrewd, albeit momentary, awareness that one cannot always have it both ways:

> '[t]he neo-liberal project of procedural justice cannot be made fully compatible with socialist ends' (Plant, p. 74);
>
> 'the satisfaction of human needs through the equalisation of positive freedoms ... will normally have an adverse effect on total income' (Abell, p. 89),

the main drift of the market socialist project is that everything men of good will would like to do to society is feasible and painless; that 'building socialism' does not commit us to the application of any particular and possibly objectionable tool of policy; that various market socialist objectives do not clash; that anything desirable that some existing type of modern social organisation – capitalism, genuine socialism, social democracy – has accomplished, market socialism can accomplish at least as well, while managing to spare us the particular nastiness proper to each; in short, it too is undertaking *so much* that it would almost certainly fail in all.

It, too, makes a triple promise. *First*, under market socialism there would be substantial equality of material conditions among men, and it would be achieved not *against the grain* through the crude levelling of outcomes, but procedurally and *with the grain* through abolishing capitalist property rights, equalising opportunity and positive freedom. *Second*, unlike in genuine socialism, individual choice would be given pride of place both in politics, by entrenching electoral democracy, and in economics, by conceding consumer sovereignty within a merely indicative framework of planning. *Third*, semi-automatic resource allocation by reliance on the market would ensure the material ease that can give us both the rising private consumption prized in capitalism, and the wherewithal for copious public provision of welfare.

'A Dull Mumbo-Jumbo'

Genuine socialism comes reciting a dull mumbo-jumbo, it is often hard work to decipher its propositions and proposals, and it carries the staggering handicap of having been tried in many places. For all the discredit practical failure has heaped upon it, however, it has the modest merit that each of its promises can be given a meaning, and that two out of the three may be mutually consistent. Market socialism has no such intellectual saving grace. The volume of essays that provoked the present paper is on the whole poorly and in places appallingly reasoned. It is astonishing to see on it the Clarendon Press imprint, reserved for works of original research and scholarship, and implying that it must have got past the Delegates. Yet the average market socialist tract is not much better argued, though perhaps less incongruous as to pretensions and performance. Plainly, advocates of a new kind of socialism have an implausible case to plead, and their chief fault is to imagine that it is a natural winner.

Genuine socialism shelters its reasoning within a private language where definitions and meanings adjust to the needs of the good cause. Social democracy carries little ballast by way of doctrine and is not in the habit of worrying about intellectual consistency. In the discourse of market socialism, however, favourite and pivotal concepts, 'social ownership', 'equality of opportunity' and 'equal positive freedom' among them, prove under scrutiny to mean either nothing or something else altogether, often something that is in the same breath expressly disavowed.

The new type of 'genuine-lottery' market, socialism's untried secret weapon, the guarantee of capitalist efficiency in an environment of 'distributive justice' and 'producer democracy', fares worst of all. It must get producers to compete in order to set roughly right prices and quantities, but must not be allowed to reward or punish them for it, for doing so is society's political prerogative. Reduced to a pretence without consequences, it is supposed to generate prices and shift resources, and 'efficiently' at that, despite important kinds of exchanges being banned and others transformed into a charade for lack of real-life owners having real stakes to exchange.

Never did a political theory, in its eagerness to escape the liabilities of its predecessor, put forward so superficial an analysis and so many self-contradictions, as market socialism. Nor does any single market socialist promise, let alone two, never mind all three – an efficient market economy without capitalist ownership, equality through equal opportunity without imposing equal outcomes, and free choice without freedom of contract – look capable of being fulfilled, each being an open contradiction in terms, much like hot snow, wanton virgin, fat skeleton, round square.

Further Reading

Epstein, R. A. (1985): *Takings: Private Property and the Power of Eminent Domain*, Cambridge, Mass.: Harvard University Press.

Hayek, F. A. (1949): *Individualism and Economic Order*, London: Routledge & Kegan Paul.

Kirzner, I. M. (1973): *Competition and Entrepreneurship*, Chicago: University of Chicago Press.

Lavoie, Don (1985): *Rivalry and Central Planning: The Socialist Calculation Debate Reconsidered*, Cambridge: Cambridge University Press.

Okun, Arthur M. (1975): *Equality and Efficiency: The Big Trade-Off*, Washington DC: The Brookings Institution.

Sugden, R. (1986): *The Economics of Rights, Co-operation and Welfare*, Oxford: Blackwell.